Happy LGBTQ

~~Pride~~ Month
Wrath

timothy arliss obrien

other works by timothy arliss obrien

Dear God I'm a Faggot

They

The Poet Heroic - a podcast

Piano Effigies - an anthology of piano music

Composers Breathing - a podcast

The Gazing Ball Tarot: a guidebook

Happy LGBTQ ~~Pride~~ Month WRATH

Happy LGBT ~~Pride~~ *Wrath* Month
Timothy Arliss OBrien

© 2020
www.timothyarlissobrien.com

"can the martyr bury
the hatchet...

after slitting
his own throat
with it?"
-me

contents 7

.someone told me to practice writing. 8

Poems for the rainy days, 11
lyrics we could sing , 25
and verses for the end of the world. 37

I'll always keep writing: 51

Nightmares, 69
haunted poems, 81
and prayers. 91

Once I was a poem! 104

But now in conclusion, 106

    I'm angry, 107

        but want to love you all. 109

            t.

prologue:

"it's true that this book was written about someone..."

.someone.told.me.to.practice.writing.

maybe I just need to forget everything I know.

you know?

I feel like *success* is a cat chasing its tail,
        not ever really coming
                to the understanding that it isn't something
 that happens to you,

    or
something one must achieve,

        but simply
                an opportunity one has
                      and decides to take or not.

pushing for my own success will
        take sacrifice
                and compromise
                      and negotiations.
    Barters,
        Trades,
                and selling my soul
                      to the devil.

¿is that what people think i've done?
(i fucking wish. that sounds fun!)

envisioning my own success is
        probably pretty important creatively,
                and habit refines craft.

what else could be as important
        when it comes to owning our
                successes and failures.
        (or any combination thereof in the realm of possibilities)

listen,
        i really think i should kiss you.

                it would clear my head a little
            and give me a slight peace of mind.

I can live with my mistakes. I can keep them like little thorny bushes in the backyard
                              behind the porch, hidden in spring
by the blooming wisteria off the back fence,

Yet still blossoming small deep satin
                roses in the late summer.

I've never smelled something so rich and sweet.

                please tell me it's possible to live with all these mistakes.

because i can't stop thinking about them.

Poems for the rainy days.

My egotistical TED talk

A young fan asked me this morning
        if I ever plan on getting Lasik,
(because apparently my glasses
                make me look inauthentic.)

You see it got me thinking...

If I could preview the future
        to make only "profitable" decisions,
              the world would be quite dull.

It certainly would make drug experimentation
and addiction
        less dramatic.

I try to pass through two liminal spaces
      every day on my commute.
 It guarantees excitement,
        and I enjoy watching people mill about.

Knowing that everyone is as submerged in the
throngs and the bustle of life as me
        is comforting.

This has been a reminder to *Be Kind* to your friends.

        Thanks for coming to my TED Talk.

LOST THINGS

I love lost things.
Because they evade all the rules of capitalism.

They can't be bought or sold.
They aren't currently of value or use,
    since the previous owner has
        processed the grief of loss and moved on
                              to replace or do without.

                But they can always be found.

Sometimes by the owner, to whom loss impacted,

      and other times by someone lucky,

Like a little miracle.

Now if only I could find myself
        just as suddenly and miraculously.

Life makes us happy

You see I was so desperate for a newness, a fresh
opportunity, I was ecstatic to snatch up
                     any option presenting itself to me.
     No drug was too strong, nor lover too intimidating.
I was hopeful of the future, don't get me wrong;
I just wanted to breathe
        and be proud with the sun warming up my chest.
    But I couldn't breathe here.

It's alright. My time had come;
           life promises to make us beautiful,
                   we just have to meet her halfway.

✻✻✻

The bad days are only inconvenient.
The heartbreak and sadness purge the heart,
             making more space for happiness.

You see, life wants to find us happy, and rub our backs,
    when we have to walk down an emotionally rocky trail.

Here is to us making it, life pouring us
                a glass of champagne and saying,

"It's ok to enjoy this moment, this season; and not worry."

                Life can be ever beautiful.

✻✻✻

✳✳✳

Her face was eager and desperate for a fresh opportunity, an ecstatic spark in her eye,
    willing to snatch up a close companion,
                      or promotion:
anything really.

    Her every breath inhaled hope, puffing out her chest to be warmed by the sun. Her complete image was striking and beautiful, life meeting her halfway with promises, but keeping her approachable and relatable.
    She would mention her bad days, but always stated that, "it's only an inconvenience!" The gleam on her face screamed,

"heartbreak and sadness purge the heart for oncoming happiness!"

Tonight was all hers.

    "Life wants to meet us happy, and rub our backs when we approach a side trail," she gushed during the toast. "Here is to us making it and life pouring us a glass of champagne!" She elevated her glass revealing the cursive tattoo on her arm covering scars and years of hatred:

Life can be ever beautiful.

the lady in the leather jacket*

"Ten quid for the violet pies sir!"
It was true she was just a snob at the zoo,
        But today she had bated some new guys.

"My self hatred is linked to the confusion
        of who I am."
"I do things just because I do them. I am me."
        She muttered to herself.
"I need to stop prescribing my parents'
 and others' dreams for my life onto myself."

She had left the cafe in a jif,
        and as shame overwhelmed her,
              the taste of honey flooded her vision.

She passed a large puddle in the city street;
reflecting the skyline and the blue overhead
        like a sheet of glass
              left for someone to fall through.

The nib of the pen scraped the paper
                as she sold her souls to the devil.

She took a bow to her Id.

*written with assistance from a random word generator game.

Sun*

Because I could not rise for Sun,
       it did kindly rise for me.
Does the Sun make you shiver?

                      does it?

I cannot help but stop and look at the dusty,
                entire earth.

  Down, down, down into the darkness of the entire earth,
Gently we go - the dust-covered,
       the dirty, the unclean.

Pay attention to the sullen sky,
       the most cloudless sphere of all.

Does the sullen sky make you shiver?

                                  does it?

Splendid sunshine is, in its way,
                      the warm air of weather.

Splendid sunshine - the true source of sizzle.

*written with assistance
       from an artificial intelligence poetry generator

Midnight train

I'm sliding
        All across the seats
                Of this express train
                        From Brooklyn
                                To Harlem
              Tonight.
Full of wine.

                    I'm drunk with you
        But not as drunk as the lady across from me
                Sleeping on her luggage.

Probably missing her stop twenty minutes ago.

The less fortune beg others for pocket change,
While the suits read the paper
        After a long day
                (high skyscraper)
                        in Manhattan.

Girls in cocktail dresses

    spill off the platform onto the train

        and giggle at boys

            they are bringing home from the club.

Nightlife,
                evading a night fright,
                                and moving past
    scratched lottery tickets under toe.

I just want to get home...

But this train has been stalled
                              for fifteen minutes.

With poetic imagery spilling
                        from all these commuters

            into our shared space.

#cancel.the.sweltering.summer

How would we go swimming
                    with Debi Toni
                            If we cancelled summer?

The rubber ducks
                    Would sit frozen
                            In the above ground pool.

As the cats sit warmly and cozy inside.

                But instead of a summer cancellation,
I'm on the Long Island Railroad from Manhattan
                    to my own spring oasis,

In a pink swimsuit, with my husband.
                        So I can be my own rubber duck.

In this sweltering heat.

a perfect day during poetry month, in the Lan Su Chinese Garden

"Fast moving brook,

        And fish swimming wildly,

                I could waste all day,

        Sitting watching idly."

<u>The Feeling of Love</u>

The ham is baked in the oven
        at 365° for one hour and fifteen minutes
                resulting in a perfect decadent candy

      we feed to each other.

This perfume carries notes of
        magnolia, peppercorn, and almond
                in a sweet bed of patchouli gardenia

to express the rich sweetness

            I can match to your shirt collar.

The song permeating the concert hall,
        rises and falls by the string quartet
                as I recognize a melody
          you once whistled

on a late night urban adventure

            in the rain.

Ginger's Curry

That mother almost left her bouquet in the booth
      at the Thai restaurant,
but her father never would let her
      leave anything behind.

And every time the door slammed shut,
      our booth trembled viciously.

A young couple fed each other spring rolls
      across the room,
and I wish I could remember us being that carefree,
young in love.

And every time the door slammed shut,
      our booth quaked with monstrosity.

Two hipster dudes shared a joint at the picnic table
outside the window,
          before devouring their shrimp pad Thai,

And every time the door slammed shut,
      our booth crumbled into the ground,
          and the whole restaurant smelled like weed.

But it's all ok, because that was the most vibrant bouquet,
the smoothest joint, and the tastiest spring roll I had ever
experienced, and I now know true joy exists.
The beaming faces of all those happy people in that Thai
restaurant prove everything will be alright.

And the red curry special with fried salmon is so delicious it
eases any issues.

lyrics we could sing

Turn on the mic

I want everyone to compose music.

I want everyone to paint.

I want everyone to ingest literature
faster
than they
                can breathe.

We are doubtlessly familiar with destruction,

                yet it is creation so many of us evade.

Not only the simple spontaneous
                creative act of procreation,

but the laborious quest to craft,
            to sculp,
                to compose!

Turn on this mic,

so I can show you the fireworks I'm capable
                of creating.

      t.

The Green of Your Eyes*

The color of kelp

Floating in the sea.

The color of moss

On a rock in a storm on the coast.

The color of a forest

During a crisp spring twilight in May.

A patch of grass

Just freshly mowed,

A neon light

Showing where to go.

A reflective street sign,

During a midnight disorientation.

The perfect color.

The only color.

*previously published in They,
and the inspiration for
  the violin composition
       of the same name.

https://youtu.be/eaaXRHbJm-g

*the joy of youth**

I wanted this piece to be as conceptual
    and playful as possible.

performance instructions:
The pianist is to start by composing a phrase
    or melody on sadness.
The pianist should then expound on this melody, or phrase
    basing their research on the studies of Fibonacci, or the
    studies of Pythagoras.

After several minutes expounding upon their melody the pianist is to pause, leaving the melodies and harmonies unfinished, and recite the following spoken word:
"Fuck this existential dread ruining my life….
(Pause)
    always making me rethink my intuitive desires."

The pianist is now to lay their head in their folded arms across the piano in defeat.
They then spend several minutes here weeping at various volumes into their arms.
Once they are able to compose themselves, they end the piece by standing, moving to center stage, and bowing.

I hope you are able to channel your inner wit, humor, and satire through this piece, and with art music.

tim <3

*premiered at the
FLUXUS2019 festival
Cardiff, Wales
by NewCELF

https://soundcloud.app.goo.gl/
ss1Rma5nBdnxS7XX6

*8100 Polls**

Stuck.
Indoors.
Inside.
    Stuck.
    Locked in a cocoon.

https://distrokid.com/hyperfollow/
banaduandtimothyarlissobrien/8100-polls

They've taken eighty one hundred polls from the people
Near and wide.
******

But we are still out of control.
A census gone rogue.

Lost in space like our ancestors,
    and forefathers before them.

We are full,
Filled to the brim,
    A symphony without song,
    A song without music.
With a need for adventure,
A need for victories.

8100: the angels number,
Of connecting,
Of relationship.
    But we are quarantined alone, together.
******
You can find us searching the cosmos,

Looking for answers,
Looking for purpose,
Looking for ourselves.
        Looking for a melody.

*Recorded spoken word performed with Banadu

A storm on the coast

A storm on the coast,

                              The city just drowns.

A community rebuilds,

                              The hurricane decimates everything.

A migration inland,

                              The scorching earth causes starvation.

A return to the sea,

                              The tempest surges.

                A storm on the coast.

https://youtu.be/_EQt16FlBlo

The Art of Finding Rest

Sometimes when I can't sleep, I imagine
I imagine I'm a boat,
                            tossed by the waves and winds.
            I imagine I'm a poppy, *I can't sleep,*

I imagine I'm a poppy, I'm in a field with sun;
                                basking in the sun.
            Sunshine.

I imagine I'm a doll, loved by a child,
                            carried alongside. *Befriended.*
Sometimes when I can't sleep,
                    sometimes when I can't sleep,
          I **dream**.

I had a dream last night I died,
                            and left my love behind.
I wasn't there to hold that hand,
                            to pick up, or keep awake.
We used to laugh,

                          I had a dream last night,
A dream, that *I died*.
Sometimes when I can't sleep, I imagine,
                      sometimes when I can't sleep,
                              I **dream**.

an experience in coming out

quartet of queer revolt

Timothy Arliss OBrien

.:prelude[1]:.
(an entrance to realize who you are)

I. ~~being~~ EXPOSITION
expose yourself to the world

>a descant for violin

<to ease our shared trauma>

II. Glide Along.^{drown}
& try not to sink!

~~give yourself~~
>"a moment to think"[2]

Let It All
III ½ thaw \'tho\ verb

in conclusion:
An epitaph[3] for solo cello.
|^|
to who they wanted me to be

---

[1] A foundation that supports and enriches the harmonies and textures of the quartet.
[2] A lullaby to support and embrace the listener.
[3] An inscription heard from my bedroom window.

A string quartet,
To express our rage.

We *will* come out,
And change this age.

Homophobia can't withhold,
Who we were meant to be.

We will overcome, and emerge,
(Stronger than ever) you'll see!

A revolt on the horizon,
And equity for all!

We will live our truth
And bigotry will fall.

So listen to the strings,
And let your hearts sail!

For today is a new epoch,
And from now on love will always prevail.

https://soundcloud.app.goo.gl/e3vCqff6NrRkiedP6

Sad rap. *

"...oh my god lil fag tears, cry me a river"

Spent all night at the bathhouse.

        I fucked six guys and I'm still out.

        Taking shots, 4am, still lonely. In my bedroom.
                              Still sad rap.

It's still that sad rap

        It's still that sad song

                that keeps me in that down mode.

        So I'll just smoke this loud though.

        So I'll just smoke this loud though.

            bong.rip.soundeffect

https://distrokid.com/hyperfollow/lilfagtears/sad-rap-single

Fuck I'm so depressed, I don't think I can go on.

Strawberry diesel, you know my whip is scented.

Yes of course I'm faded,
                                  It's not my fault you're jaded.

It's that sad rap
          it's that sad flow it's that sad state
                                      that I always go.

It's that sad rap
          it's that sad flow it's that sad state
                                      that I always go.

                    Yeah of course I'm faded

It's that sad rap
          it's that sad flow it's that sad state
                                      that I always go.

It's that sad rap
          it's that sad flow it's that sad state
                                      that I always go.

                                      that I always go.

*Recorded and sung by Lil Fag Tears.

and verses
for the end
of the world

Setting little fires

I'm setting little fires in my house,
       in my heart.

I think we got to this point,
       because I needed to stay warm.
Not just in my blood and bones,
       but in my soul.

I need to know what you think of me,
       and if you approve.

What's the worth of existence without one's own happiness though?

Maybe you should stop setting fires in my house,
       my home ablaze,

           and keep your opinions
                    to yourself.

Red Dawn *

Black sky to blue.

Oblivion and peace of mind.

But alas, the crimson clouds warn of fright.

Soon enough, the tempest looms.

The destructive storm terrorizes,

Obliterating all in its path to rubble.

Maybe sky to turquoise.

                Shining down on *destruction*.

*previously published in Deep Overstock issue four:
                                      Nautical Lore

Carnivals

Rattle.

Screech, rattle.

Panic ensuing, everywhere.

Ghosts.
Terror; vermin.
Children drowning.
      (In cotton candy/asbestos)

Carnies.
Shadow-lurking.
Secret smoke spots.

Bubblegum

(on a)

Rat's foot.

It climbs the wall.

Things That Are Hot

- the Sun

- My stream of morning piss against
                                            the porcelain bowl

- My burning rage at the homophobes
                  trying to convince me to commit suicide

- The summer sand, basking my body
                              by the shimmering river

- The bath water,
              waiting to soothe my aching bones

- My spouse and I's hearts,
                  beating wildly as we lay, chest to chest,
                in the afterglow

Two Cowboys Holding Hands *

Many had complained to the Sheriff
But those two were still
              mocking this whole rodeo.

It was a strong gesture, an impassioned move.
They were even rumored
              to say they loved one another.

Many in the community just said
              they needed wives.
But they just kept going "home" together
                      to the same farm every night.

      Once, in the middle of the hottest summer on
record, a few of the guys from the stockyards drank heavily
at the tavern and tried to burn down their barn.

      But this was the day the town chose
hope, kindness, and love.

For you see, the community remembered all the things those two cowboys had done for them. Once they herded up a whole head of dairy cows, that had escaped the Double "O" Ranch. Another time they had fixed a two mile fence that had been damaged during a late spring tornado right in the middle of town.

These were good cowboys, and this town knew the difference between a hero, and a villain.

The cowboys spent all winter fixing their barn together. And marrying inside, in front of the whole town that spring.

The arsonists were charged

                and spent life behind bars.

Because no one harasses a good cowboy,

                or a couple of them.

*previously published in Deep Overstock issue six:
                                        Westerns

Who Do I Get to Fuck?!

If I fuck 100 people,

Who the hell am I hurting?

The one hundred?
Or just me,
The one?

Tabitha Acidz's trip to the lake *

Tabitha takes a trip at the lake.

It wasn't the best LSD she's ever obtained,

But the effects were real
    and they shook her to the core.

"I swear I have a psychic connection to animals now" she boasts to the bartenders and go-go boys on Saturday evenings.

        "The mushrooms from Gary are the best,
If you hit it just right you can
                converse with Jesus, and the saints"
she told her sister over Sunday morning brunch.

    Tabitha's psychedelic obsession almost ended her career:
        she was searching so hard
           for something that was within her from day one.

You see the reality was,

Tabitha was just a sad little boy,

In a dress,

Looking for beauty in the world.

*written in memory of the time I met Tabitha,
        after drinking the angel tears she sold me,
                and becoming my favorite drag queen.
Premiered in The Poet Heroic Episode Six

Empty Cupboards*

The desolation started during the pandemic.

Lines at the bank
    wrapped around and around the block.

For some it was their first encounter
    with the demon of food insecurity.

The young ones cried
    carrying around an empty stomach
        for God knows how long,
While the parents whimpered
    embarrassed as headlines labeled them
        failures.

Others hoarded supplies as normal.
    More than enough to overflow their plates,
        their houses,
            even their silos.

The angels looked down in disgust
        as they counted resources,
                knowing there was plenty
        for every hungry mouth and yearning stomach,

        while supplies rotted in the fields, untouched.

The seraphim begged for the creator to intervene,
        and stop the destruction
                of His most precious sculptures,
"I've tried, they've refused my help
        and won't love themselves, each other."
Was all the almighty everlasting would echo.

"If only they could share," said Saint Peter,
working tirelessly at the golden gates in the clouds,

        granting reprieve
                and entrance
                          to lines and lines of casualties

        wrapped around

                and around

                        the block.

*previously published in Deep Overstock issue nine:
                                            New Arrivals

Drunk on vodka and seltzer

A grandfather clock
And a stopwatch,

Walk into a bar,
And order a shot of tequila for each other.

Who know which blacks out first,
And who knows,
Which can keep time.

But the drag queen at the bar,
Has the tallest hair in the county,
And no one can blame a black-out,
For all the expletives that are
Screamed into the mic
This Saturday night.

Tonight I'm drunk on vodka and seltzer,
Living my best life,
Knowing I've drunk too much,
Swallowed one too many loads,
But I'm happier than I've ever been.

Please don't call me,
I won't answer,
And don't leave me a voicemail,
I won't listen to it.

Tonight is a night I don't want to remember,
For it was far too perfect,
And I don't want to
Set an impossible bar for the future,

I love you,
And no one can take tonight from us.

Viva la August twentieth.
2020.

Death *

Little drowned creature

Fur so shining and wet

You only wanted across the street

But now look what you get!

Death.

* in memory of a poor drowned rat trying to cross the road
                                                           to get to the Goodwill

I'll Always Keep Writing

I'll always keep writing

How could I possibly stop writing?
I've been writing and composing music since I could read.
Kids books are essentially glorified poetry.
Short sentences, and bright vivid storylines.
I used to obsess over the paralleled colors
and bright word choices.

I guess the only thing that changed is my content.

My early education provided me with some pretty shit teachers. (and even crappier administrators)
The Cottingin's year was by far the worst, and the brutal bullying was the least of my anxieties. (Bullying to the point of my desk being moved to the front chalkboard of the class, right next to the teacher's desk)
The reek of ferrets would meet me at the door each morning, dreading the moment the small beasts were released from the torturous cages.
On one of the more terrible days, with the poor creatures crawling over twelve children, one of my aggressors started chanting:

gay Timmy
Stupid faggot
kisses boys,
kisses ferrets.

Soon the whole class was joining in,
   And I was off to the principal's office.

   But this injustice of homophobia was not what made this teacher the worst. For you see, this teacher had us all writing short stories, which I loved to do. My imagination would run wild, and I could unleash my sense of adventure on the page and create my own world:
               no limits.

   For some reason, this teacher hated my writing. He would also let us color and draw, and create our own "book covers" and illustrations.

         he.also.*hated*.my.art.

   The kids that year got to make wonderful booklets of their short stories, self illustrated and bound to perfection.
   Unfortunately, I was not included in that project, and at the young age of 11, I was devastated. But I did keep all my stories and hope to publish them some day as children's books.

   I was lucky enough to have four poems in a class anthology that year, *Seasons*, *Winter Turns to Spring*, *Pets*, and *I Do Not Understand*.

Seasons

Seasons come and go,

Winter snow is before us.

Fall leaves are behind.

Winter turns to spring.

December

fridgid, dull

snowing, wind, beach, kites

skiing, swimming, scorching

green, colorful

June

Pets
Dog

huge, funny

pouncing, playing, eating

fun, fur, cuteness, purr-fect

walking, sleeping, eating

loveable, pretty

Cat

I do not understand

I do not understand...
    why we are alive
        and not just molecules on another planet.
    why we cannot go to another galaxy,
        why everyone isn't just alike.

I do not understand...
    how we can live on earth, be the only lifeforms,
        in all of outer space.

What I understand the most is...
    how small we are   compared to outer space.
I do not understand
        how many black holes are there?

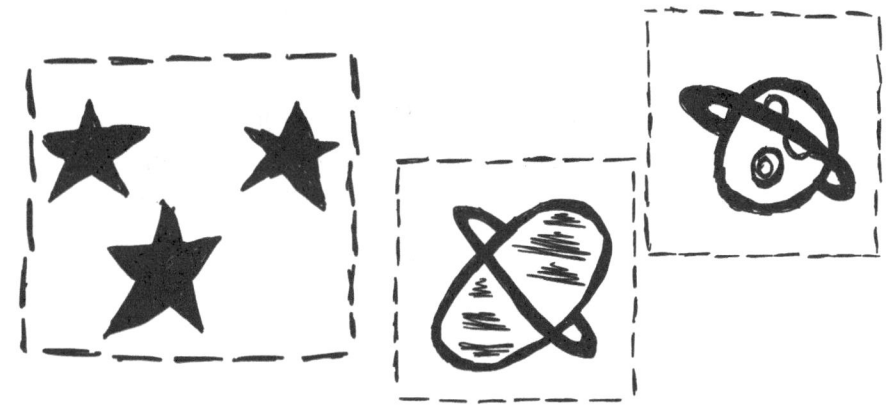

The middle grades were an animal I was able to tame. The academics excited me and I blossomed as a reader, digesting every John Grisham thriller I could get my paws on. I was determined to become a Supreme Court justice.

I wanted to bring rightness and order to an unfair and chaotic world. The bullying continued, and several of my peers would taunt me and constantly call me a fag.
I had one enemy who would name call me all through class so one day I threatened to stab him with my safety pin if he didn't fuck off.
I got in school suspension for a week.
He was never reprimanded for anything.

Even though I found erasure of myself once again from society, in my music I often found escape from my lack of social engagement. I would sit in band and lose myself in the shared harmonies we would create together, composing in my head: How *I* would **create** the music.
And nobody could bother me when we were all blowing hot air through metal and wood. (although there was one bully in the percussion section who would torment me endlessly. Maybe that is why I compose such difficult percussion parts.) Fuck drummers, *amirite*?

I had forgotten my love of writing these years, but had a very special teacher who would constantly improvise writing prompts and encourage us to submit the results to competitions.

That's when I truly understood my poetic gift
and how I was published in A Celebration of Young Poets:
from the Heartland (Fall 2002)

<u>Friends</u>

They make me feel loved.
They are always nice no matter what.

They never leave my side
                              even in times of trouble.
They never insult me
                              even when I act out.

They protect me in times of danger.
They stand up for me in times of need.
They like me for who I am.

They are always there.
They make me feel loved.
They are there when I feel:
depressed, sad, mad, or happy.

They forgive me
no matter what I do.

They are my friends.

High school brought an onslaught of sexual frustration and rage at the multiple bullies pushing me to the brink of suicide. I knew that there was a way to exist as a queer person in society.

It meant affluence and relocation to a politically blue state.

I cannot pretend I had an easy time with family, but I felt the need to push people away, hide who I was and protect myself from any dastardly deed of homophobia that might be lobbed my way. I'm sorry Mom.

During my Junior and Senior years, I found refuge in myself and the music, art, and writing I could create. I also found confidence and comfort in the many brilliant teachers I had, who not only believed in me, but challenged me to do my best with the resources I had.

I spent hours with a brilliant artist, who taught me perspective and color theory. I learned language from several wonderful teachers, who helped me with my structure and flow. And my obsession with music exploded in many piano compositions and several arrangements for the band.

Those geniuses, completely brought the best person I could be, out from within myself.

My college prep school was demanding and the technical academics so often didn't leave room for my creativity, although I thrived in all of my arts classes. (AP English lit/lang, AP Music Theory, AP Studio Art, and strangely AP Biology)

Usually I slept through English period, because I typically snuck out most every night, (to drink, experiment with drugs, or entertain cute guys) only to sneak back home at four or five in the morning to get ready for school.
(Sorry again Mom)

I was still able to speed read all my assigned books in a matter of days, write essays on the spot that received high marks, and maintain an A in the class.

The constant partying and escapism through drinking threatened my diploma, but I was able to rally with teachers to pass the troublesome classes I just really couldn't be motivated to be bothered with. (AP U.S. History, AP Government, AP Chemistry, and AP Calculus)

For senior year, I wrote a trilogy of poems to escape the world that was tearing me down. Rejected by over ten publishers, I have always been proud of this burst of imagination I created.

Timothy's Trilogy

Part one: Ode to Aurora

The lightning is a cobweb in the sky.

As I touch the snow I can:
Smell the fire,
    See the pain,
        Hear the screams.

        Maddie performs tricks in California,
And no one in the world is beautiful,
    Because of that time you kissed me.

The dull paint of pain,
        makes me jump off the edge of the world.

For tomorrow when we are old,

    We will
        Still be
            Funny, smart, and beautiful.

But tomorrow is the past
        that no one today will forget.

So when the rocks come out of hell,
And the clouds cry with grief,
We WILL forget tomorrow.

But tomorrow is just an illusion.

While smart songs are playing in our heads,
        And as Aurora dances in her mirror alone.
            We are as beautiful as the dead.

But songs don't play in our head anymore,

    and we don't feel beautiful.

    And now waterfalls, mountains, buildings,

                  and snow,

        Keep us apart.

      But we will never be together

The sadness smells the way a chalkboard
                  feels under my feet.
And we walk on chalkboards
                  on our way to hell.

Because Aurora isn't dancing in her room
        for anyone, anymore.

Part two: "I Love You"

Spit on my face you stupid whore,
                                       in that space by the barn.

I wish I were thoughtful, beautiful, and innocent.
                                   Innocence: only for the naïve.

I wish I had a boat
         So I could go for a walk.

A brightly colored boat
         Like the green of a stoplight.

I'd cut my hair myself
         Because I know that we can't have a home.

The boat is covered with ideas
         And we know we can succeed.

                 Let us live on it and call it a home.

But you love land soooooo much :(

It's such a shame how we live
                            It's such a shame that our boat sank.

It's a shame we still love each other
                It's a shame that you had to have that surgery.

The vet said you would live through it.

I guess it's time to name you,
        And bury you in the backyard,
                Like a dead goldfish.

And say a prayer
                                              to Jesus

                because he will save us.

Part three: Lie To Me

My Mustang was a Lumina

And there was rust on the hood.
Just like that rabbit I hit with that stolen tractor.

His little rabbit body lay limp
                          His fur as soft as a baby chicken.

Smelling his death,
      I heard a shriek from the woods
            And tasted the blood as I bit my lip.

His little eyes looked,
      Like the sound of a spring waterfall.

Rhonda drove into Colorado ,
                          In that rusty Lumina,
Before that wreck with a stolen tractor.

            But "no one" hit a rabbit there.

And
Time is on nobody's side
And
Lust is something *no one* falls for,

Because we had open heart surgery
                                            on the same day.....

The green grass of love,
Grows like the waxing moon around us at night.

She ran to me and took my hand
            And we flew through the sky towards
That girl Aurora we thought we knew so long ago.

Soon we will know everything
                                       and never be wrong.

      Baby lights leave us naked in the sun,

            So that by the time we stop walking,
      We can name
Every single star

                  As if we had lived there.

Even though my college years were fraught with electro shock ex gay therapy, and a constant barrage of rules, regulations, and denouncing others due to their sins, I maintained a fierce relationship to writing.

Whether it was required bible devotions that were published to prove I had forsaken same sex attraction, or poems on tear stained pages in my private journals,
(many of which are contained within this very book!)

I never stopped writing.

So I hope Dr. Cottingin is rolling over in his grave, at the success this troubled faggot has created,
and I *forgive* him.
And every other terrifying homophobe who has hated themselves so much, and been so scared of authenticity, that they have had to vilify the victim.

and I'm through being the victim.
(go bet on it)

How could I possibly stop writing?

Because to write is to understand,
to indulge in self awareness, to know thyself.

So how could I stop writing,
when I think the best way
we can be kind and love ourselves,
is to know one's self.

I'll always keep writing.
t.

Nightmares

The fishing incident*

An oath taken at dawn
In light of the bright sun
cascading out of the ocean
An oath to tell no one

Not even thy self
A secret that shall die at sea
And stay at sea
The lifeless wet body
Slumped over the bow of the boat
Slippery and wet into the black abyss.

Half man, half fish.

He had stopped breathing seven minutes after being
pulled in with the net.
Seven minutes of pure bliss, with the most beautiful
creature I have laid eyes upon.

An oath at a funeral,
happening too soon.

*previous published in Deep Overstock issue four:
                                        Nautical Lore

Little Blazes

Roam the forest looking for little blazes,
Sprouting up around the best of us,
Threatening to burn our ecosystem down.

Quickly,
Stomp them out,
Quickly now, hurry!

My heart is getting hotter,
And I fear I may not outlast this fever.

Come rescue me,

My dear firefighter,

Please come save me

Quickly now, hurry!

The Past

I hadn't the memory to conceptualize what it was like in the foster home when I was five months old, but the pictures give me a splice in time that shows me small paneless windows into the past.

I had never really been provoked to look into "little baby Jeremy", the name I was called before the adoption, but when the magic man with the mystery time box came into town, I became curious. My friend Evangeline said he could take me back in time and I thought it could be a really fun experiment, or a waste of a day.

Tickets were $270, but I had money saved up and had been a little bored with school and work. I needed some excitement in my life.

I showed up at the old rusty warehouse and muttered to Evangeline something about how with ticket prices this high, this magician should get a better venue.
The rust and unplaceable chemical smell assaulted my nose instantly and I was so taken aback, I hadn't even noticed the early start of the process of jumping through the pictures in my hand.

The old man was wide eyed and muttered to himself often, but I followed him to a small desk and laid out the pictures. I was standing in front of a snapshot that depicted an older gentleman holding a small fragile baby and talking on a toy telephone. He had me lean in closer to the picture, almost so close that my nose was touching it, and describe to the audience the scene.

The air was crisp by the pool side and the gentleman smiled mid hearty laugh, with a residual cough showing he had been a longtime smoker, but had given up and was now feeling better.

The sun rippled off the small blow-up pool in the background, as kids ran around the large yard, splashed in the pool water, and the old man exploded in jolly laughter.

I heard a dog bark and turned my head with a shock, realizing the warehouse had dissipated and the warm sun roasted the back of my neck. A dog ran up to me and warmly welcomed me to this new paradigm.

"Hey there!" shouted the old man, "I'm so glad you came back to fill in some memories." He strode over to me, while holding baby Jeremy. "I knew you would come to see how your first few months of life were, they all come back eventually."

It was warm and this beautiful place made me never want to leave.

The old man smiled like he knew what I was thinking.

"Others have stayed and made this home. You can too!" He said with the warmest smile and brightest gleam in his eye.

I hadn't seen that much joy in the world

                                                in a long time.

Memories From Oklahoma *

The wild Wild West isn't so wild anymore.

It's now mostly parking lots,
                            suburbs,
                                            and shopping malls.

But I did fuck a cowboy once.

His horse wasn't as big as he said,
               and I would have mistaken it
                           for a petting zoo donkey in a parade.

Idk how he could take it to the rodeo.

                            And he was terrible with a lasso.

             At least on *me*.

But who would be able to lasso me?

I'm the 21st century Wild West:
     Weed, psychedelics, and new age philosophies,
         Conquering the vast plains of the sub-conscience.

Maybe I just fucked a cowboy to brag about it.

*previously published in Deep Overstock issue six:
                                                        Westerns

Will it to end

A dream.
But a waking nightmare,

A tear stained breakfast each morning.

"Will it ever end"
She screamed with a hoarse voice
                                    and salt covered cheeks.

The dishwasher

I want to buy a new dishwasher,
But there's nothing wrong with the one I have.

It simply does not match the room,
                And is much too cacophonous at night.

I used it with a few bricks inside,
        Hoping it would give me an excuse,

But all it did was flood my house,

                And now I have to move!

The adventure of the ice cave *

The ship left port all too late at dusk.
Sailing 36 km due north for the ice fishing spot.

I had traced the location of a lore-based deep ice cave only half an hours journey west from the popular ice fishing spot.

Legend had it, that contained within was a crown, that when worn would bestow the powers of weather. The ability to cause storm and tempest, or with the right planning, paradise. Crops watered properly, and fair weather for all.

Halfway to the fishing spot, a thick blizzard started falling straight down, as if someone was trying to prevent our journey.

We reached the fishing spot extremely later than anticipated, but in one piece.

The hike for me was effortless, as I had been preparing for a decade, snowshoeing at every chance.

The old manuscript, left to me by my grandfather at age nine, denoted that the stairwell would be located between two bastions of ice. And they would triangulate with the highest peak into a perfect isosceles triangle.

I reached the two pinnacles, walked straight between them and started digging.

It took me ten minutes to hit stone; all too soon for the amount of snowfall. The stone was the first step and soon I had dug out ten.

After the fifteenth step, my way was paved with crystalline walls of ice and frigid air.

I soon lost contact with time and seemed to fly down the stairs faster and faster.

After an indeterminate amount of time, I realized I was surrounded by a glow and the ice was melting. I started pressing against the walls and soon they were collapsing away revealing a large ice cavern, fathoms deep and wide.

Molten lava ran like rivers deep below me, as skyscraper sized stalactites dripped into the smoldering earth.

I could see a raised part of the earth with a crafted pedestal of ice jettisoning upward. I peeked around the corner of the ledge I sat on and was horrified at what I saw.

Frozen little creatures covered in feathers bustled around the ice pedestal carving and polishing it. A huge ice sculpture of a man rose out of the pedestal. Atop his head was a golden crown, encrusted with sapphires and rubies.

At that exact moment, the earth started to rumble and a deep voice called out, "Who tresspasess here? Leave my cavern at once!"

I could hear the small creatures squawking and scurrying about, looking for me, I presumed.

Running upward on melting ice stairs that had previously been stone, proved to be a challenge. Although I did gain about fifteen steps up before slipping and striking my head against the wet melting ice wall.

I was told upon waking, six months later, that I was found clawing at the snow four days after our ships departure. No sign of hypothermia, muttering to myself about becoming king.

*previously published in Deep Overstock issue four:

                 Nautical Lore

Just a sad poet

I just can't stop crying.

And no one can understand the poet.

"I consider myself a poet first and a musician second. I live like a poet and I'll die like a poet." Thanks for seeing me, Mr. Dylan.

And why is the poet always a suicide? Why do the "best words in the best order" as Samuel Taylor said it, eat me up inside "and it makes my whole body so cold no fire can warm me... as if the top of my head were taken off" as Dickinson put it.

Too many wordsmiths die by their own pen-held hand. Whether in an oven door open, or in a river with a pocket full of rocks.

I hope I don't meet the same fate,
And I can exist with this deep sadness
For years to come.

Simplicity

The small moments always lose me. I want to be in the sky, amongst the Pleiades: Ad astra per aspera.

And there I'll find myself, among the stars.

Whenever I act up I say, "Tim you better knock it the fuck off!"
Because if I don't succeed, I'll never be happy.

But Edwin Morgan won the Queen's Gold for all of his dreams and nightmares,

So why can't I want the same?

Because if I'm not happy, I'll never succeed.

Maybe one day I'll be able to dedicate a poem to an opening of an LGBTQ center,

But honestly all I need today,

Is one cigarette.

haunted poems

Undoing a curse*

I knew since long ago,
    a curse walking into,
        on a Saturday morning.

A reflection from a shattered mirror
                  the night before,

the curse crawls up,
    from the abyss,
        bald,
        210lbs,
and way too old to exist.

It knocked me out,
    with a bloody face,
        in the morning.
It burned down three Thai restaurants,
    and leered over my shoulder,
                  of a coffee shop,
      all afternoon.

By the spill of my red blood,
    and this red ink on paper,

May I be free:

    a broken mirror, a bloody face, and the bald abyss,

        staring straight through me

*previously published in Deep Overstock issue seven:
                      Horror

That Van Gogh Cow Cart

That dreary cow cart
       haunts my vision.
              (looms over my self-slaughter)

Jesus Fucking Christ,
      my hands are numb.

To quote Hunter S. Thompson,

           "I'm done with games."

A lone car alarm drones on outside,
                        cutting through the downpour.

The oven door was left open,

                        tempting my head for sure.

I'm too chicken shit to keep a pact
              like Sid and Nancy,
                  but still bury me in my leather jacket.

Honestly,

            no two people could have been happier.

The Mailman

Bryce the mailman skirts across the street like it is a pond and winter has come early enough for everyone to be cheery.

But the letter he was entrusted to deliver would only bring heartache, trauma, and turmoil.
The accursed post was meant to harm the receiver and enact revenge for a generation long feud.

This small envelope will fall the leader of a dynasty, and its riches would be dispersed to the less fortunate.
Redemption for those always manipulated in the shadow of the great thought king.

Bryce moved rapidly to be done with the dastardly deed, weaving between houses, mailboxes, planting empty blank envelopes randomly on his journey onward. To throw off any trackers.

    But only blocks from completing his mission, Bryce was
                              Suppressed by an assassin.

Ending his mission for good,

                              Because sometimes, the evil win.

The Betrayal

It was under these cherry blossom trees
                                        that they betrayed me.

Shot me out of a cannon, and left for dead?

Who knows what would have happened
                    if I had chased that car
                                  after that dreadful hit and run.

The Bad Guy

Unknown to the good around me, I am evil.

The treacherous voice within me
                            is an onslaught of self-saboteur.

The hugs I give, and condolences I share,
are void compared
                          to the villainous selfishness in my vision.

Blinded by fear and terror,
I must take care of self.
The bad guy shows up and gets his agenda done.
He receives his justice, his portion,
                          by his own morals, his own laws.

Gone again, it's just us good guys.
 Just don't piss me off,
                          and I'm sure the villain won't return.

Asp-bite & river rocks

A haunting, a long avoided reunion...
Lost over centuries.

I wasn't there when she sank into that dark cold
flowing silt soup.

Words struck silent,
and a vision extinguished.

(Did anyone hear the world fall quiet that day?)

The serpent's venom stilled the heartache, that was
too much for the poor queen.

A demise still remembered,
Century upon century.

A thousand new lovers
in the next year

I want to meet a thousand new lovers in the next year.

I saw a hearse on my walk home after we fucked
        and it made me wonder, "how am I gonna die?"

I hope it's in your arms, or his, or hers, or theirs.

I can't think of something more tragic
        than dying all alone.

The moon seems closer this time of year,
        and the air is so cold sometimes
              I can barely see.

But I know you are there beside me
        because I can hear your breath.
              And feel the rise and fall of your chest.

Roman told me last week
        that he didn't want to live anymore
              but I had texted him just in time.

A subtle serendipitous reminder, that we all mean something to someone, and we are very often coming to someone's mind.
        And someone will always think of you,

So please stay alive today,
        Maybe you can become
              one of my new lovers this year.

The milkman

A church Sunday.

Leather print and handcuffs. Distraction.

Squeaks out of a purse.

Screaming.

The pastor's sermon baked at 350° for two hours:

    Burned.

Roasted his heart to death by adultery.

The Letter Poltergeist

Dear self,
I wanted to pen a letter to you.
A letter that outlined my emotions. A letter unapologetic...
A note on sorrow and on fear...
I don't think I can succeed.
    My spelling is shit and my typewriter is broken.

Forgive me, please, I didn't choose this madness,
        rather it chose me...

Please send help for I don't think I understand myself
fully. My conscience has been a wild fox full of conquests.
You think you see me,
but the reality of the situation is clear,
You see right through me.
John: don't tell me to behave
   Mary: please speak softer, you know how easily the baby
                                       wakes

I'm the baby, sent to save us all.

I hope this letter finds you well,
        and you have prosperity the rest of your days.

Write to me more frequently, as I do miss hearing updates
        from your extravagant trips.

Love and respect,
        T.

Prayers

From Steven: to live in sexual perversion. It is tragic.

"To live in sexual perversion. It is tragic." -steven*
*the pastor who performed electroshock ex-gay therapy on me

Yea...
It's also 😵 so tragic 😵
That you felt the need to invade my inbox
                                              with your opinion,
Which I
            did. not. ask. for.

So here's the deal Steven,

  You gotta tell me what you want...

Me to divorce my husband,
                    (because God told you to tell me)
me to unpublish my poetry and rescind the art expressing
my lived experience,
    (electroshock therapy chapter and all?)

Or do you just need a hug
                 and someone to pray with you
                                through the shame?

You see,

                        You gotta decide what to ask for,

And then if I decline,

              Opt-out,

                            Or say no,

      You gotta just leave it at that dude.

I pray to our God

                that one day

                        happiness will find you too.

Amen.

I Have a Dream*

The other night I had a visceral dream.

And
                        My banner was ten feet tall.
Enshrined upon it was *God Loves Everyone*.

Rainbows dropped from it,
                             as I stood blocking evil.

             For you see
             Behind me

Was a banner reading: **Fags Burn In Hell.**

The hatred spewed from the banner
                            and angry bigot holding it.

The name calling and void-of-love
                                 burned my ears,
Yet,

I endured through the whole parade.
                 Teaching others acceptance and love.
A queer nocturnal heart cry.

Because,
                 I have a dream!

(Tell them about the dream Tim!)

I have a dream,

                        That one day,

The world will have equity and acceptance,

                                  for all my queer family.

A world so full of love

                        there is no space for homophobia.

**ature*I still have that dream.*

.:amen:.

*previously published in Deep Overstock issue five: Dreams

On Faith*

Have you ever been confused
                             about where life is taking us?
                (*Assuming we are in this together.*)

I had a dream I met with a really great pastor.
She was more concerned
               with my spiritual and emotional wellbeing,
than with my theological knowledge.

But I have always struggled
                       to have a place at Christ's table.
            Most churches turn us away.

Because our marriage bed is sinful,
         Because my commitment to him is apostasy,
                Because I chose to say no to hating who I am.

      A guitar plays slowly in the background, squeaking and
                        sliding past all my self hatred.

I want my heart to be as soft and delicate
                          as the dahlias on the altar.

             Lord Jesus make us brave.
                                            Amen.

*previously published in Dear God I'm a Faggot

A poem to the pastor who tried to shock the gay out of me.

No!
You can't
Keep me here

        Afraid.
        Hating myself
        Wanting to change

                Scary
                It seems
                to be alone

        But I must
        Do something
        Anything

Alone?

        Not I...

            I have God's love.

        Amen!

On sanctuary*

The faith that I puff up,
    with my steps through the door.

The hope that (so often) dwindles,
    as my queer soul prepares for judgement.

      Gay heart in the house of God.

My feet collect all the broken glass
          on the city streets outside.

And I rest my broken bones,
    in the light of your countenance,

        and *grace*.

Restore, and make me anew,
    that I might love,
        and accept myself,

        as you have done
          for me.

Amen.

*previously published in Dear God I'm a Faggot

<u>A Poem By Timothy:</u>
<u>to my previous bible college.</u>

Dedicated to the university
    where I received C-PTSD
    after trying to be cured of homosexuality
        and then kicked out like a stray dog.

Mental torture.

    Hypocrites everywhere.
    Congregating in cesspools.
    Masturbating their ideas violently onto others.

Someone.

    Please,

        Stop them!

Amen.

A God Ordained Relationship

Dear God,
    I'm a faggot,
        but I still believe I deserve simple graces.

I deserve an honest, inclusive faith community,
    a choice in acceptance.

My lover does not deserve any shame,
                my husband.
My religion nor my sexuality define me.

    I *deserve* to define myself.

Sometimes I don't want to speak,
    for fear,
        for embarrassment.

I didn't notice myself cross a line,
    by holding his hand,

        hands adorned with our marriage bands...

But still they throw rocks,
                and hurl judgemental insults.

Tell me God,
                shall I remain quiet?
                              (*unobjective?*)

Or shall I douse myself in gasoline
                and make a **public display**?

I'll still hold his hand around the homophobes,
            my husband.

They may revolt against our marriage,

        But they can't take away our relationship.

A relationship given by God.

            thank.you.and.amen

on being queer*

Dear Queer Christian,

You are mountains tall,
               and brave.
                        You are rivers and valleys deep,
        And lovable.
You sit inside a chasm that looks into one land,
          and *yet* peeks into another.

We rally at dawn against the self righteous,
               Valiantly, and nobly.
Warm dawn,
               Dewdrop on grass-blade,
                   and mist from the river,
                           Under our footsteps.

God has built his throne upon us,
     The Church,
          God's beloved. God's children.

We were beautifully and wonderfully made,
                 And God's works are awe inspiring.

We do
               Know this well
                              Amen.

*previously published in Dear God I'm a Faggot

a world of peace

Peace peace peace!

they cry for stillness,

But the rage in their hearts burn with war.

If only by a passing chance
all could accumulate enough love
to stifle the hate in this world.

We,
by divine graces,
could taste such harmony,
and such peace.

amen

Once I was a poem

This is one of those long impossible nights.
 I want to drive a long way from you.
I just want to leave and keep on going.

I already miss you.

I lose all my ex lovers
and want to just stay on the road and keep moving.
The nights are getting colder and quieter.

I really don't have enough money
                for a hooker, for a pet, or even for friends.

Donate my organs to someone more hopeful than me.

      I found a tooth on the ground while I was walking to a
bookstore. I overheard another sidewalk person say,
   "He bummed me the fuck out and that's why I left him."

            Is that what *you* think of me?
Now that we share our beds with other people...

What is the courtesy one should act
                when someone buys you a drink but you are sober.

I was walking down the street
        and I saw the bus run by
                and it just attacked me.

I can't understand how to tell you better
        but the baby fell out the window of the bus

so as I move and breathe
I can understand that some people really look for a future
        when they're going in a certain direction
but no
no

I don't see why you can't understand where I'm going.

I really want to make it to a place in my life
      where we can walk past the convenient store
and the people that are shouting will shout out our accolades
          and move their minuets in a way that claim the sky.

I saw her go to the bathroom and she never came back
      I don't know if she died in there
      or if there is something else that I should know happened.

I don't know
      but our dinner came
          and it got cold
      and once it was cold I didn't know what else to do with it

      but put it in my briefcase and *walk* away.

Sometimes when I'm walking I get lost
      and I just keep walking
          because I'm lost
and what's the point of walking unless you know
                  where you are going

so I just laid down in the street
      and I see the cars pass by
the buses speed by

and I get offered drugs
      and I take the drugs
          because what is the point of being sober

when you don't know where you're going.

I'll give you a little advice

      don't say no to drugs

      because this is an experience that we all deserve.

But now in conclusion,

My laboured breathing
                      into anxious lungs that are fucked

    Between stressed shoulders:

I contain a heart of war with itself - full of anger.

    But beating with resilient hope.

I'm angry,

but
I want to love you all.

T

Timothy Arliss OBrien is an interdisciplinary artist in music composition, writing, and visual arts. His goal is to connect people to accessible new music that showcases virtuosic abilities without losing touch of authentic emotions. He has premiered music with The Astoria Music Festival, Cascadia Composers, Sound of Late's 48 hour Composition Competition, and ENAensemble's Serial Opera Project.

He also wants to produce writing that connects the reader to themselves in a way that promotes wonder and self realization. He has published several books of poetry (Dear God I'm a Faggot, Happy LGBTQ Wrath Month, They), several cartomancy decks for divination (The Gazing Ball Tarot, The Graffiti Oracle, and The Ink Sketch Lenormand), and has writing featured with Look Up Records (Seattle) and Deep Overstock: The Bookseller's Journal. He has also combined his passion for poetry with his love of publishing and curates the podcast The Poet Heroic and he also hosts the new music podcast Composers Breathing.

He also showcases his psychedelic makeup skills as the phenomenal drag queen Tabitha Acidz and expanded his love for music by transforming into the up and coming SoundCloud rapper Lil Fag Tears.

Check out more of his writing,
     and his full discography at his website:

          www.timothyarlissobrien.com

I would like to thank every person who helped me make this book possible. My full gratitude to the universe for my precious kitten Chloe, for always sparking my imagination and teaching me to play. My undying love to my husband, the best editor I'll ever meet, and always my favorite composer. (No two people will ever be happier.) None of my publications would have been possible without my parents, who have always believed in me, supported me, and celebrated with me in my every achievement. Many thanks to the countless friends and family that have been there with me for all the years, and my wonderful supporters through Kickstarter who made this publication possible.

You all help me keep my creativity alive.